LADYBIRD BOOKS

UK | USA | Canada | Ireland | Australia

India | New Zealand | South Africa

Ladybird Books is part of the Penguin Random House group of companies

whose addresses can be found at global.penguinrandomhouse.com.

www.penguin.co.uk   www.puffin.co.uk   www.ladybird.co.uk

First published 2023

001

Written by Libby Walden

Illustrated by Ekaterina Trukhan

Copyright © Ladybird Books Ltd, 2023

Printed in China

The authorized representative in the EEA is Penguin Random House Ireland,

Morrison Chambers, 32 Nassau Street, Dublin D02 YH68

A CIP catalogue record for this book is available from the British Library

ISBN: 978–0–241–56733–3

All correspondence to:

Ladybird Books, Penguin Random House Children's

One Embassy Gardens, 8 Viaduct Gardens

London SW11 7BW

WISE ABOUT MY BODY

Written by Libby Walden

Illustrated by Ekaterina Trukhan

So, what's in the book?

Welcome to
Wise About My Body

Everyone has a body. Your body is your first and your forever home.

There are over seven billion human beings on the planet and they **all** have a body. But not all bodies look the same, and there is no body quite like yours.

Your body is incredibly special because it is the **only one** like it in the

whole world.

This is your guide to how bodies work.

It is your guide to how bodies move.

And it is a guide to how bodies should be looked after.

In fact, this book has been written to show you that your body, the place you live and sleep and breathe, is

amazing!

What is a body?

"Body" is the word we use to describe the whole structure of a human being – from the moving parts hidden away inside to everything you can see on the outside!

Your body is made to last you a lifetime.
And as you grow and get older,
your body will start to look different.

Things might happen in your life that change the way your body looks.
But it will **always** be **your** body!

We have lots of words for different parts of the body –
both inside and out. Let's take a look at a body from the outside first.

Can you point to all the different body parts
on the children below?

NOSE

EYE

HAIR

HEAD

EAR

MOUTH

CHIN

NECK

HAND

ELBOW

SHOULDER

STOMACH

THUMB

FINGER

CHEST

ANKLE

FOOT

LEG

KNEE

TOE

ARM

What can a body do?

Not all bodies are the same. Some people have disabilities that restrict their movements. Some people have illnesses that mean they can't do everything all the time. But here are a few things that the body can often do:

GROW

A body can change shape and it can grow. It might get bigger, taller, fitter or curvier.

FEEL

Your body helps you to experience the world. It might help you to feel textures and temperatures. It can help you to feel emotions, like happiness and sadness, and even to feel pain.

AGE

With each birthday, you get older – and so does your body!

REPAIR ITSELF

If you fall and get a cut or a bruise, your body will work hard to repair itself. If you get ill, your body will try to fight the sickness so you can feel better.

MOVE

Your body is your own personal vehicle! Bodies move in lots of different ways – they might run, jump, skip, stretch and crawl.

We look different!

Human bodies have lots of different features.
The body often has two eyes, one mouth, ten toes,
two legs, two arms, one nose but lots of bodies don't.
Our bodies all look different – and that's why they're beautiful!

Human bodies come in all
shapes, heights and sizes.

Human faces might be
wide, narrow or round.

Skin might be different shades and textures.

Eyes might be grey, blue, brown or green.

Hair might be afro-textured, curly, wavy or straight
and some people have no hair at all.

Lots of people use aids, medicines
or machines to help them experience the world.

Our differences make us special, and all bodies
are beautiful – whatever they look like!

Genius genes

Lots of things can affect what we look like,
from what we eat to where we live. But the biggest
reason we look the way we do is our **biology**.

Your biology is the set of natural characteristics that you share with
people you are related to, including your biological parents.
These **natural characteristics** are called **genes**.

Genes are tiny pieces of information that we get, or inherit,
from our biological parents before we are even born.
They help to decide what we look like.

As genes are shared between people who
are related to each other, people in the
same family who are related might look
alike or at least look similar to each other.

Do you look like your parents, grandparents, brothers or sisters?
You might see features that look like yours, but you might not!

Families aren't always biologically related, and even when
they are, they can still look very different.

Inside a body

A human body is a natural, whizzing, whirring machine.
But inside our bodies we don't have cogs, wheels or pistons.

Instead, we have amazing natural
elements that are connected and
work together, without us even
realizing that they are there.

Our bodies have hundreds of moving
parts that work together, around
the clock, to keep us healthy
and to keep us alive!

Here are some important things we all have inside our bodies:

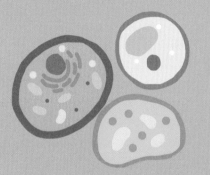

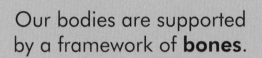

Every part of the body is made up of millions of tiny building blocks called **cells**. Cells are microscopic, but they make and look after EVERYTHING in our bodies.

Our bodies are supported by a framework of **bones**.

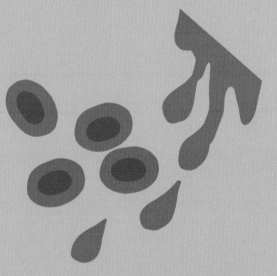

Muscles are made up of stretchy, elastic strands called **fibres**. Muscles help us to move, flex and bend.

A special liquid called **blood** travels all around the body. It transports things our bodies need, like **nutrients** from food and drink or **oxygen**.

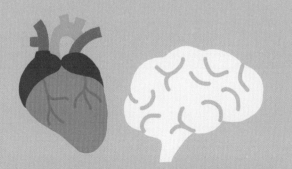

Our **organs** are large working parts, and they all have very important but very different jobs.

Strong skeleton

Your body is given shape by a framework of bones.
This framework is called a **skeleton** and everyone has one.

The skeleton **supports** your body and **protects** your organs.

Bones are very light but together, in a skeleton, they are
strong enough to support the weight of the whole body!

All the bones in our bodies have special names.
Here are a few important ones to know.

SKULL

The main job of the skull is to protect the brain. The skull is made
up of 22 bony segments and gives our faces structure and shape.

SPINE

The spine is a long chain
of 26 special bones, or
vertebrae. It runs down
the centre of our backs.
Our spines give us
support and flexibility so
we can move around.

RIBCAGE

The curved bones that are found in our chests are known as ribs,
and together they make up the ribcage.

The major organs

Your body has lots of different large working parts called **organs**. Organs work together to keep you alive and healthy, and each organ has its own important job to do.

Let's take a look!

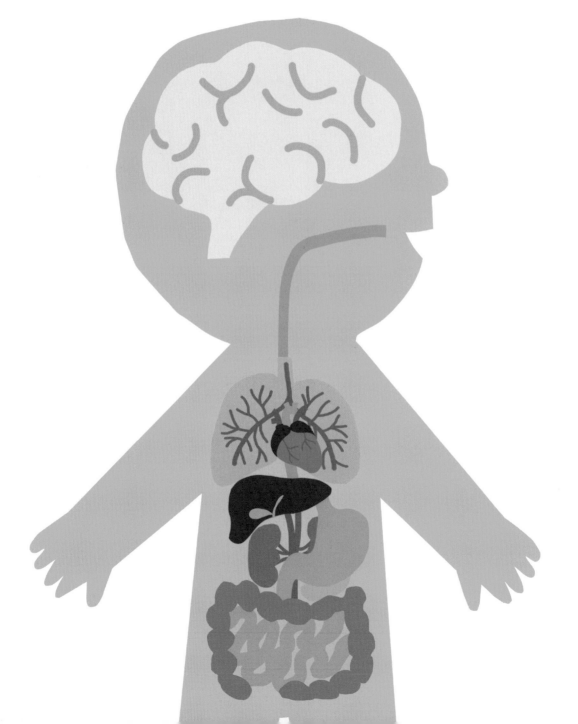

The **brain** does all of your thinking and it tells the rest of your body what to do.

The **heart** is a big muscle that pumps **blood** round your body.

Lungs help to bring fresh air into your body and release waste air from your body.

The **stomach** helps your body to break down food into smaller pieces so you can soak up all the useful nutrients from everything you eat and drink.

The **liver** stores all the energy for your body that has been collected from the food you eat.

Kidneys filter the blood, removing any waste or extra water and turning it into wee, or **urine**.

All the solid waste from your stomach is fed into your **intestines** so you can get rid of it as poo!

Brain power!

Hidden inside your head is an organ that is in charge of **everything** your body does. It works like a powerful computer, and it is on all the time, even when you're asleep.

It is the . . .

brain!

Your brain is connected to the rest of your body through cells called **nerves**. Together, these nerves make up a network called the **nervous system**.

Nerves constantly ping messages to the brain from the rest of the body. The brain processes the information, decides what to do, and then sends a new message out into the body with instructions on how to respond.

But the brain is not just one big messaging system.
It is responsible for so much more!

Your brain stores all your MEMORIES.

It is where your RESPONSES and FEELINGS come from.

The brain is responsible for BALANCE and MOVEMENT.

And it helps you to CREATE ideas, paintings
and stories using your IMAGINATION.

Magic muscles

We have more than 600 muscles in our bodies and they all help us to move. Muscles are made of strong stretchy **tissue** that makes our bodies powerful and flexible.

There are three main types of muscle.

Cardiac

muscle is a special muscle that moves the heart, pumping blood through the body.

Skeletal

muscles are attached to the skeleton by cords called tendons. These are the muscles we use when we move around, and they give us power and strength.

Smooth

muscles control the movement of our organs.

Your face has lots of muscles under the skin. They help you to laugh, cry and even pull silly faces. You use 17 muscles to smile and 43 to frown – try it and see!

The strongest muscle in your body is found in the jaw. It helps you to chew lots of lovely food!

Your muscles have memories – sort of! If you practise an action over and over again, your muscles will get used to that movement and develop **muscle memory**. This means that they will work more precisely and get better at that movement.

Making moves

There are lots of different ways to move around.
We might move our bodies by running or crawling, skipping or hopping. We sometimes move without even thinking about it, perhaps when getting out of bed, nodding our heads or waving to friends!

So how do our bodies **move**?

The brain will send a **signal** through the body to the muscles that are attached to the skeleton.

Muscles are connected to bones by stretchy cords called **tendons**. So, when the muscle moves, it moves the bones as well.

When a muscle gets the signal to move, it either **shrinks**, which pulls the bones it is connected to together, or it **relaxes**, letting the bones move away from each other.

The place where two bones come together is called a **joint**. When you move a knee, ankle, shoulder or elbow, you are moving a joint in your body.

Your brain then works with your muscles to keep the movement going.

There are lots of ways to move your body. Movements can be tiny, like blinking your eyes or wiggling a finger, or they can be huge like a cartwheel or a jump.

The five senses

We use our bodies to find out about the world around us.

There are five **senses** that can help the
body to make sense of its surroundings.
You might . . .

HEAR with your EARS,

TASTE with your TONGUE,

SEE with your EYES,

TOUCH with your SKIN,

SMELL with your NOSE.

When the body picks up a new smell, discovers a new taste or hears a new noise, it **collects information** for the brain.

For example, if you touch something hot, the **nerves** in your skin will send a **message** to your brain, letting it know that you feel pain.

The brain will then organize the information and send a **reaction** back out into the body. It will tell your muscles to **move** your hand away from the heat and out of danger.

Sometimes people are unable to use one or more of their senses. Glasses, hearing aids and ear defenders are just some of the devices people can use to help them understand the world.

How the senses work

All of our senses are controlled by the brain. The brain uses the information collected by each sensory organ to interpret and identify the world – so you could say we hear, taste, see, touch and smell things with our brains!

HEAR

All noises travel through the air in waves, known as **soundwaves**. The ears act like funnels, collecting noises and guiding them inside the ears, where they become vibrations. These vibrations are then turned into messages and sent to the brain.

TASTE

If you stick out your tongue and look in the mirror, you will see lots of tiny bumps on the surface. Most of these bumps are **tastebuds**. These little sensors tell your brain if you are eating something sweet, salty, bitter or sour.

SEE

Eyes use **light** to see objects, which is why it's easier to see things in the daytime! As light bounces off different objects and enters the eye, the images are focused, turned into electric messages and sent to the brain.

TOUCH

The skin is covered in tiny sensors called **receptors**. These help you feel things, from the wind on your face to the fur of a puppy. The information detected by your skin receptors is then turned into a signal and sent to the brain.

SMELL

Smells travel through the air and enter our bodies through our **noses**. The nose can detect around 10,000 different smells.

Brilliant blood

If you have ever fallen over and cut yourself, you might have seen a red liquid come out from inside your body. This liquid is called **blood**, and it does a very important job.

We need blood in order to stay alive and healthy.

Blood travels all around the body, delivering oxygen and nutrients everywhere it goes.

It also takes away waste from the organs – that's anything leftover that the body doesn't need – and fights off infection.

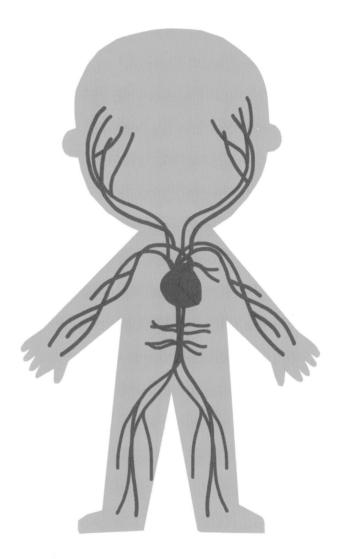

Blood gets round the body through a system of tubes, or blood vessels, called **veins** and **arteries**.

What is blood made from?

PLASMA is the liquid part of the blood. It is a yellowish fluid that carries the cells round the body.

PLATELETS are repair cells. When you get a cut, platelets will rush to the area and build a barrier to stop the bleeding. This is a process called clotting.

RED BLOOD CELLS give blood its red colour. They carry oxygen from the lungs, delivering it through the body. The more oxygen the cells contain, the redder they are!

WHITE BLOOD CELLS help to protect the body against illness and disease. They travel through the blood on patrol, looking for bacteria, viruses and infections!

The heart

Sitting in the middle of your chest is your body's powerful pump – the heart.

Make a fist with one of your hands. That is roughly the size of your heart!

It doesn't look that big does it? But this small, muscular organ works non-stop to keep you alive, pumping blood round your body every minute of every day.

Your heart beats roughly 100,000 times a day, which is around 3.5 million times a year!

Hearts are very powerful but complicated organs. Hidden inside a heart are four areas, known as **chambers**. There are two chambers on the left and two on the right.

Blood moves through the heart in one direction. It fills up the top chambers of the heart, then muscles squeeze it into the bottom chambers and then out into the body.

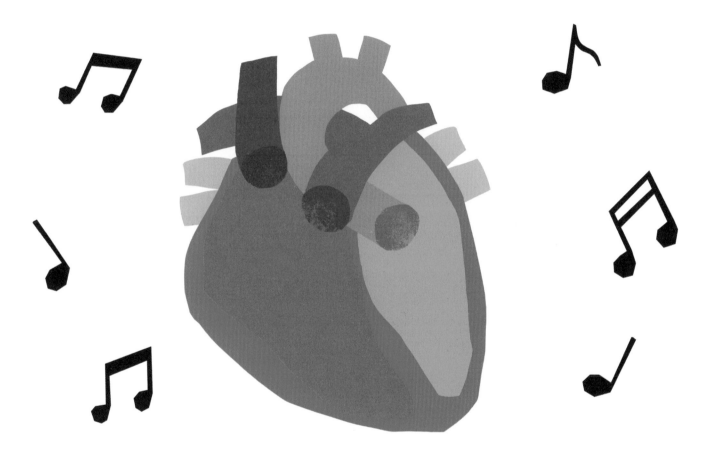

Little doors, called **valves**, open and shut to make sure the blood travels through the heart in one direction.

When you listen to a healthy heart, it will make a *duh-dum* noise. This is called a **heart beat**, and it is the sound the valves make when they shut as blood moves through the heart.

The lungs

Our bodies need air to survive.
A gas called **oxygen** is found in the air around us, and our bodies use oxygen to turn the fuel from our food into energy.

Two organs, known as the lungs, help us to get air into our bodies. The lungs are found in the chest, under the ribcage, on either side of the heart.

Air comes into your body through your nose or mouth.
It then travels down a tube called the windpipe and into your lungs.
We call this action **breathing**.

Your lungs are important tools that also
help you to talk, sing and shout!

There are stretchy muscles in your throat called **vocal cords**.

When you push air from your lungs past the vocal cords, they
vibrate and help you to make a noise. You then use your
mouth, jaw, tongue and lips to shape the noise into words.

Breathe in . . .

Put your hand on your chest and take a deep breath in.
Did you feel your chest rising?
Now breathe out.
Did your chest go back to normal?

Your lungs are like two balloons. The more air you put into them, the bigger they get. So, when you take a BIG, DEEP breath in, your lungs get bigger and they need more space.

A special muscle sits underneath your lungs. It is called the **diaphragm**.

When you breathe in, the diaphragm moves down and the other chest muscles move out, giving the lungs the room they need to fill with air.

breathe out

When you breathe out, the diaphragm moves back up and your chest muscles move inwards. This pushes the air from the lungs back out through your mouth and nose.

We breathe in and out all day and all night, often without even thinking about it. On average, a human will take about 22,000 breaths a day!

Staying alive

There is an amazing network of organs and blood vessels built into your body. This system delivers oxygen and nutrients to all of your cells and removes waste and waste air, known as **carbon dioxide**.

When air enters your lungs, the **oxygen** in the air is collected by tiny sacs in the lungs called **alveoli**.

Each one of these tiny sacs is covered in a mesh of **blood vessels**, which are filled with blood cells waiting to absorb the fresh oxygen.

This blood then travels to the heart and is pumped out into the body through blood vessels called **arteries.**

As blood travels around the body, it releases oxygen to the organs and cells and collects waste products the body no longer needs.

This blood is then returned to the heart through blood vessels called **veins.**
It is pumped back to the lungs on a mini circuit to receive fresh oxygen and then returns to the heart to be pumped out again!

The skin

The largest organ in the body is the skin.

Skin covers every part of the body, holding everything in place and keeping the organs, bones and muscles hidden from the outside world.

The skin protects the body, allows the body to sense things using touch and helps to keep the body at just the right temperature.

Skin is beautiful in all shades, from pale to dark. It can vary in colour on the same body, have features like raised dark spots called moles, and even become darker in the summer after time in the sun.

Hot and cold

Our skin is very sensitive to change, especially change in temperature. Here are some things that happen to our skin when we get hot or cold.

When the temperature gets hot, the skin tries to cool the body down as quickly as possible. It will allow blood vessels to grow big and flow closer to the surface of the skin. It also starts to release water, or sweat. These things help body heat to escape into the air and cool us down.

When the temperature gets cold, the skin tries to keep body heat from escaping. The blood vessels will shrink in size as much as possible, moving away from the surface of the skin in order to keep the warm blood closer to the inside of the body.

Food is fuel!

Our bodies need fuel to stay healthy and work properly.
Food is our fuel. We get nutrients from the plants and animals we eat.

It's really important to have lots of fresh food every day,
but that doesn't mean you can't have a treat once in
a while, too! How many of these foods do you enjoy?

APPLE   CUPCAKE   BANANA   CHICKEN

BREAD   PEACH   CARROT   PINEAPPLE

CHOCOLATE   CRISPS   PASTA   BROCCOLI

TOMATO

BLUEBERRY

STRAWBERRY

CUCUMBER

SANDWICH

FISH

ORANGE

PEAS

CHEESE

EGG

BEANS

RICE

All living things need **water** to survive. Water keeps the body working properly. It helps blood to flow round the body, it helps the body to get rid of waste, and it also helps us to digest food properly.

Make sure you drink plenty of liquids throughout the day, especially when it's hot or if you exercise.

Where does food go?

Food gives us energy to keep moving
and it keeps our bodies functioning properly.
But where does food go when you swallow it?

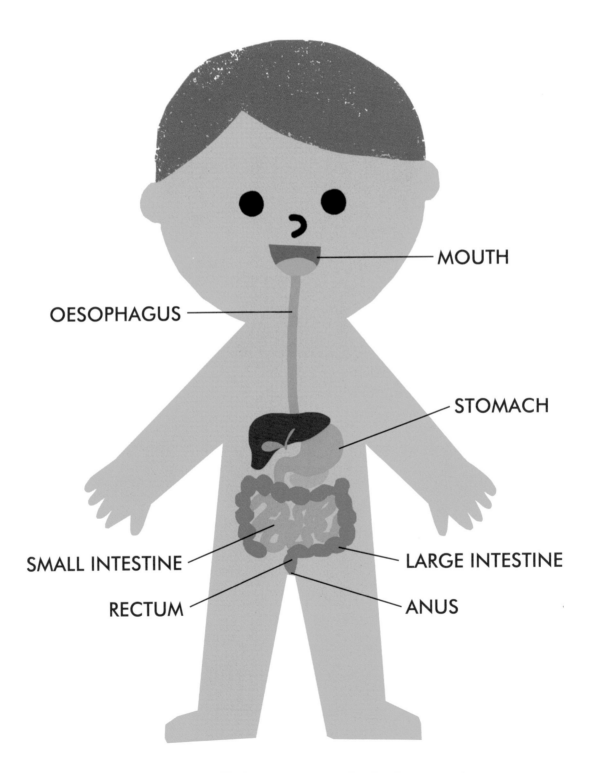

MOUTH

OESOPHAGUS

STOMACH

SMALL INTESTINE

LARGE INTESTINE

RECTUM

ANUS

When you take a mouthful of food, you chew it with your teeth and mix it with spit, or **saliva**.

When you swallow the food is pushed down to your stomach through a special food pipe called the **oesophagus**.

In your **stomach**, the food gets churned up even more and broken down into a thick liquid.

This liquid then travels into your **small intestine**, where useful nutrients are transferred into your bloodstream to be delivered all over your body.

Unwanted or waste food moves into your **large intestine**, where the water is absorbed from it and it turns into hard waste, or poo!

This poo then leaves your body through the **anus** when you go to the toilet.

Let's get moving!

Moving your body is good for you. It exercises your muscles, gets your heart rate up and gets air into your lungs. It can even make you feel happier!

There are LOTS of ways to move and have fun. How many different ways have you tried?

SWIMMING

CLIMBING

ROLLER SKATING

FOOTBALL

TRAMPOLINING

GYMNASTICS

WALKING

SKATEBOARDING

TENNIS

RUNNING

CRICKET

DANCING

RUGBY

CYCLING

JUDO

YOGA

When you exercise, you might notice some changes happening in your body.

Your breathing will get quicker as your body needs more oxygen to work your muscles.

Your heart will beat faster to move that oxygen around.

Your skin might get wet with sweat or perspiration. This is one of the main ways your body tries to cool itself down, and you might need to drink more water to replace what you sweat out!

Stay fresh and clean

One of the ways you can try to keep your body healthy is to make sure it stays clean. Bugs, bacteria and germs that can make you sick are found in dirt and love grime, so here are a few things you can do every day to make sure they stay away!

HAVE A WASH

Jump in the bath, splash in the shower, or have a rinse at the sink – just try to make sure you wash regularly!

BRUSH YOUR TEETH

To keep your breath fresh and smile shiny, brush your teeth with a toothbrush and toothpaste for two minutes twice a day.

USE A TISSUE

If you have a sniffle or feel a sneeze coming, reach for the tissues! Using a tissue will keep the germs from spreading to other people.

WASH YOUR HANDS

Make sure you wash your hands with soap and water throughout the day. It is especially important to wash them after using the toilet and before a meal.

PUT ON CLEAN CLOTHES

Try to always wear clean clothes and put on a fresh pair of underpants every day.

WASH AND BRUSH YOUR HAIR

Keep tangles, nits and dirt at bay by washing your hair regularly and brushing it often.

COVER YOUR MOUTH

If you need to cough, sneeze or even yawn, be sure to cover your mouth. This will stop germs from spreading to other people.

Feeling unwell

If nasty bugs known as germs find their way into the body,
they can sometimes make us feel under the weather.
But our bodies have some tricks to fight back!

When you get a cold, you might notice that your nose runs with snot, or **mucus**. Your body creates mucus to try to trap nasty bugs and get them out quickly when you blow your nose.

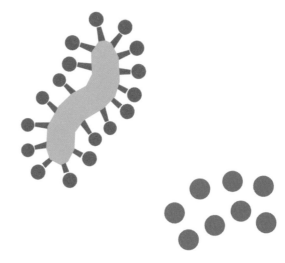

When you run a **fever** you might feel really hot. This is your body making it harder for the virus to multiply, as higher temperatures can slow down the spread of the virus.

When you cut yourself, the **platelet cells** in the blood come to the rescue! They rush to the area of the cut and join together to create a barrier, or **clot**, to stop the bleeding. This can then harden to form a **scab**.

The best thing you can do if you feel unwell is to **rest** and **drink** lots of water. Remember to always tell a parent, carer or grown-up if you don't feel well.

Illnesses can be very different, from a cold that goes away in a few days to something more serious that means you need to go to the doctor or hospital.

Some people's bodies need extra help to fight bugs, and they might take medicines to keep their bodies as strong and healthy as possible.

Bedtime and the body

Every night we close our eyes and go to sleep. Humans spend about one third of their lives asleep. Sleeping is as important to the body as food or water.

When you sleep, your body continues to work.

Your heart still beats, you breathe in and out and your brain still sends messages, but sleep allows your body to reset.

It gives your muscles a chance to relax, slows your heart beat and deepens your breathing – all useful things to relax your body and help you wake up feeling fresh in the morning!

Sleeping gives your brain time to process what you've done in the day. It helps your brain to store away all the information it has learned and helps to create memories.

Dreams are stories and images that appear in our mind, while we sleep. They can be lovely stories or scary nightmares, but they are all normal.

Humans spend about two hours a night dreaming. Quite a lot of dreams are forgotten when we wake up and often people dream in black and white rather than in colour!

Dreaming is part of the thinking process. You are more likely to dream during the time of night when your brain is most active.

Do you remember your dreams? Did you dream of something last night?

It's MY body

Human beings can be very sociable.
People often like to wave, hug, shake hands and kiss.
But just remember – that your body belongs to **you**.
This means that you're allowed to say if something
doesn't feel OK or if you don't want to be touched.

Here are some things you can say if you feel uncomfortable.

You should also check with other people to see if they're comfortable with being touched. Here are a couple of questions you can use.

What should you do if you are made to feel uncomfortable or something upsets you?

If you can, immediately step away from the situation. Find someone you trust, ideally a grown-up, and let them know what's happened. This could be:

a person in your family

a police officer

a doctor or paramedic

someone who works at your school.

What an amazing body!

Our bodies are always at work, keeping us healthy and alive.
They are complicated but interesting machines!
Here are some more fascinating facts about the body.

If you feel anxious, angry
or nervous, a **deep breath**
can really help. It slows down
your heart rate, increases your
oxygen levels and helps to
calm your body and mind.

A sneeze can travel at a speed
of up to 100 miles per hour!

The thinnest skin is on your
eyelids. The thickest skin is
on the soles of your feet.

A typical adult human has 206
bones, but a newborn baby has
more than 300. Bones fuse
together as babies grow, so we
always start out with more
bones than we end up with.

The ridges of skin on your fingertips create patterns when you dip them in ink or paint and place them on paper.
These patterns are called **fingerprints**, and everyone's fingerprints are different.

When it's cold, the body sometimes **shivers**. This is your body moving your muscles quickly to try to create heat!

The largest and heaviest muscle in your body is in your bum! It is called the *gluteus maximus* and it helps to move your legs.

Your ears never stop growing!

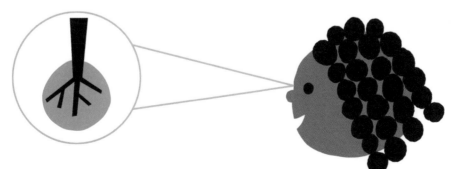

The image your eyes send to your brain is actually upside down! Your brain switches it up the right way so you don't get confused or dizzy!